Desert Bighorn Sheep

By Dale E. Toweill

Acknowledgements

The author extends his sincere appreciation to Teale Toweill and to Jeff Gould.
Their editorial skills and thoughtful comments enhanced this book.

The publisher also wishes to acknowledge staff members of the
Living Desert, Palm Desert, California, for their assistance.

Cover photograph:
Bighorn Ram

Published by

nature trails press
P.O. Box 846
Palm Springs, California 92263
Telephone (760) 320-2664
Fax (760) 320-6182

International Standard Book Number (ISBN): 0-937794-36-8
Printed in China

Contents

Introduction

The bighorn sheep is the largest native animal inhabiting the deserts of North America. To most wildlife aficionados, it is also the most imposing and the most regal. Males, called rams, grow massive horns. With a circumference of twelve to fifteen inches at their base, the horns curl back around the ears and from there sweep forward in a dramatic arc to form a complete circle of up to forty inches. The females, called ewes, also possess horns. They are nearly straight, not curled like the ram s, and at twelve to sixteen inches in length are noticeably shorter with a much narrower base.

Adding to their dramatic physical appearance, desert bighorn sheep occupy some of the most spectacular scenery in North America. At one time, they were found throughout all of North America's hot desert regions. Their existence on blisteringly hot stony cliffs and canyons, described by one naturalist as the most inhospitable terrain on the continent, contributes further to the charisma of this truly remarkable animal.

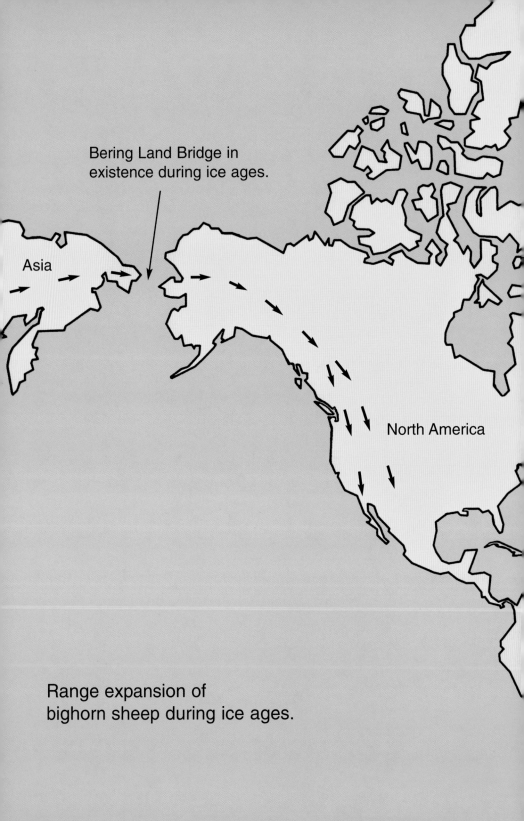

Bering Land Bridge in existence during ice ages.

Asia

North America

Range expansion of
bighorn sheep during ice ages.

In The Beginning

Given the dramatic adaptations desert bighorn sheep have made for life in hot and arid environments–living in some of the most inhospitable places in the world–it may be surprising that the ancestors of modern desert bighorn sheep were not desert animals at all. Rather they were creatures of the cold, glacier-strewn mountains of central Asia. These ancestral bighorns–blocky, sturdy animals well-suited to endure bitterly cold winters–probably crossed a temporary land bridge from northern Asia into North America as much as 100,000 years ago. While fossils of these ancient bighorns are few (rocky steep slopes and high mountain glaciers tend to pulverize bones), there is sufficient evidence to indicate that ancestral bighorns were among a great variety of mammals that occupied North America at the end of last ice age.

The world was a much different place then. Evidence of the great diversity of species present 12,000 years ago is given by bones preserved in the famous La Brea Tar Pits located in Los Angeles, California. Included among plant-eating animals were not only bighorn sheep, but many other species now extinct: long-horned bison, Columbian mammoths, ground sloths (larger than modern grizzly bears), horses, camels, long-legged shrub-oxen, and rhinoceros-sized eucatheres, which looked like a kind of super-bighorn with their long curling horns. Several varieties of antelope (including the modern pronghorn) and peccaries as large as domestic hogs were also present.

At that time, the tremendous variety of plant-eating animals provided food for an array of predators–predators that, like the plant-eaters, are mostly extinct today. Saber-toothed cats and their relative, the scimitar-toothed cats, competed for prey with cheetahs, jaguars, pumas, lynxes, and lions larger than today's African lion. Dire wolves (the height of timber wolves but heavier) patrolled the plains, as did red wolves and coyotes. Three varieties of bear, including the short-faced bear that used its long legs to run down prey, competed with the other predators for food (Geist, 2000).

Competition for food and a need to escape predators forced ancestral bighorn sheep into demanding habitat margins. It is speculated that bighorns lived near the edges of great ice-fields where lush grasses grew in soils fertilized by glacial loess and where steep, rocky slopes and icy cliffs provided escape terrain. It was selection for this habitat that destined ancestral bighorn sheep to become desert-dwellers. As the last ice age ended and the climate warmed, bighorn moved higher into increasingly isolated rocky hills and mountains to find rich forage and protection from predators. Over time, populations of bighorn sheep became isolated at the highest elevations on these mountain islands as lower elevations became arid and deserts formed. With no potential for escape as desert climates overtook even these last refuges, desert bighorn were forced to adapt-or die. Many other ice age mammals, unable to live among the rugged mountains or cope with increasing aridity, became extinct as bighorn sheep flourished.

Bighorn Ewe (female)

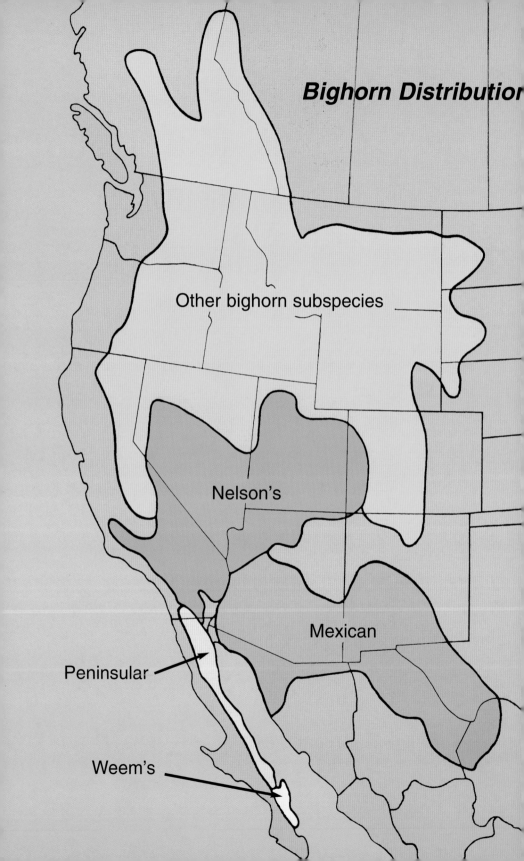

Bighorn Distribution

Other bighorn subspecies

Nelson's

Mexican

Peninsular

Weem's

Distribution and Taxonomy

The scientific name for bighorn sheep is *Ovis canadensis*, or literally, "Canadian sheep" because the first specimen to be scientifically studied by taxonomists came from the Rocky Mountains of Canada. The bighorn sheep from the Rocky Mountains are the same species as those from the North American deserts. Desert bighorn, however, are often considered different subspecies–so designated by adding another term following *Ovis canadensis*. Many mammalogists recognize four subspecies of desert bighorn sheep: Nelson's, Mexican, Peninsular, and Weem's.

Nelson's desert bighorn sheep (*Ovis canadensis nelsoni*) is the most common race of desert bighorns. Currently found in the Mojave Desert of southern Nevada, southern California and northwestern Arizona, Nelson's desert bighorn sheep has been described by some taxonomists as having a much larger range in the past than at present. According to at least one taxonomist, Nelson's bighorn historically ranged from southeastern Oregon and southern Idaho southward throughout Nevada and Utah into northern Arizona and California, and almost to the Mexican border.

Historical ranges of bighorn subspecies in the North American deserts, modified from Monson and Sumner, 1980.

It is the Nelson s bighorn that adapted to life in Death Valley, where temperatures can soar to 134 degrees Fahrenheit and where rock outcroppings absorb and re-radiate heat like solar ovens.

Mexican desert bighorn sheep, *Ovis canadensis mexicana*, are found primarily in the Sonoran Desert and to the south and west of the range of Nelson's desert bighorn sheep. The range of this subspecies includes southern Arizona, New Mexico, Texas, and the Mexican states of Sonora, Chihuahua, and Coahuila. Far less common than Nelson's desert bighorns, Mexican desert bighorns have adapted to live in some areas, like Sonora's Pinacate Range, that may be virtually devoid of surface water for years at time.

Baja California has two races of desert bighorn sheep. The Peninsular bighorn sheep, *Ovis canadensis cremnobates*, is found from Palm Springs in southern California southward, west of the Salton Sea to Loreto in Baja California Sur. Populations of Peninsular desert bighorns in California were identified as an endangered species in 1998, due primarily to the loss, degradation, and fragmentation of habitat, all associated with human develop- ment (U.S. Fish and Wildlife Service, 2000). Although some of the mountain ranges in Peninsular bighorn sheep habitat may exceed 9,000 feet in elevation, these animals typically occupy the foothill ranges from 700 to 3,400 feet--elevations that often coincide with areas of human activity. Populations of Peninsular bighorn sheep nearly always occur on dry, east-facing slopes.

Weem's bighorn sheep, *Ovis canadensis weemsi*, is found from Loreto south to the tip of the Baja peninsula. In contrast to the

Bighorn Ram

rocky and dry mountain ranges north of Loreto, Weem's desert bighorn sheep live in desert habitats that feature deep black soils and relatively abundant drinking water sources. The vegetation is characterized by often dense, semi-tropical vegetation with palo blanco and palo verde trees, organ pipe and prickly pear cacti, and several species of elephant tree.

Bighorn sheep habitat in Death Valley National Park, California.

Form, Adaptations, Water

The demands of living in a desert environment requires animals, large and small, to make adjustments in both physiology and behavior. The most obvious changes have to do with body size and shape. Large animals require more water than smaller animals, and cannot cool their body temperature as quickly to cope with high temperatures. Over the course of centuries, desert bighorn sheep have thus become smaller than their ancestors as a way to prevent overheating.

The weight of desert bighorn also fluctuates more radically with the seasons than their counterparts in more humid and more productive environments. A desert bighorn sheep ram that weighs 200 pounds in early summer may weigh only 140 pounds by winter (Hansen in Monson and Sumner, 1980). Ewes typically weigh about 115 pounds in summer (Valdez and Krausman, 1999).

More significant as an adaptation to hot climates, however, is the shape of the body of a desert bighorn sheep. Although a desert bighorn ram may stand as tall at the shoulder as a Rocky Mountain bighorn ram (30-40 inches), the desert bighorn is typically much less 'blocky' than its northern counterpart, with relatively long, thin legs, a slender neck, and long ears. These changes in body structure maximize the amount of body surface area relative to body weight, allowing blood vessels to carry body heat to the skin surface where it can be cooled by the surrounding air. The ears and neck, in particular, are useful for cooling the body because of large blood vessels just under the skin. The hair covering the body is thin in these areas during the summer, providing minimal interference with the cooling process. The sides and top of the body feature relatively thick hair even in the summer, providing insulation from the summer heat. Insulation is increased with the growth of a thick coat of underhair (fleece) in the autumn, coupled with development of a layer of fat under the skin which provides additional insulation. The fleece is shed by early summer, and desert bighorn rarely have much body fat left by the time spring arrives (Hansen in Monson and Sumner, 1980).

Physical adaptations such as these are made more effective by behavioral adaptations, such as feeding during the coolest parts of the day, and resting in the shade during the hot daylight hours. Desert bighorns have also been known to select cool rocky caves as retreats during hot weather. These kinds of behavioral actions are intertwined with the animals' physiological adaptations. For example, resting during the hottest part of the day reduces the amount of time available for feeding, reinforcing selection for a small body size that requires less food for maintenance.

The combination of small body size, body shape, behavior, and variations in weight, are all limited in what they can do to meet the demands of desert conditions. Physiological adaptations complete the story of how bighorn survive in hot and arid environments.

Two ewes, note the narrow horn bases.

Desert bighorn sheep perspire little, relying instead on the evaporation of moisture from respiratory surfaces during breathing (the mouth, throat and lungs) and energy conservation to regulate body temperature. Bighorn can also allow their body temperature to rise as high as 107 degrees Fahrenheit (Toweill and Geist, 1999), a temperature that would be fatal to many other kinds of animals. This reduces the need to use precious body water to maintain the lower body temperature found in most other mammals.

Bighorn sheep have a specialized digestive process that is very efficient in manufacturing water from the forage they consume. This *metabolic water* can replace much of the water bighorn sheep might otherwise need to drink. When water is available, however, desert bighorns can drink more than two gallons per minute, and have been recorded drinking five gallons at one time! Even when water is readily available, desert bighorns drink only once every two or three days on average. When drinking water is not available desert bighorn have the ability to withstand a loss of up to one-third their body weight due to dehydration (and recover fully when moisture becomes available).

As mentioned previously, bighorn rarely perspire. Instead, they avoid running or other activities that increase their body heat, and select the coolest locations during hot weather. Additionally, desert bighorns have developed means of reducing the amount of water lost as a result of eliminating waste products by excreting very concentrated urine and very dry fecal material. These mechanisms combine to allow desert bighorn sheep to survive for long periods without drinking. By some accounts, desert bighorn sheep can live without drinking water for as long as six months!

desert waterhole, Coso Ranges,
Mojave Desert, California.

Extremely light, albinistic desert bighorn ewe,
Grand Canyon National Park, Arizona.

Abundance and Habitat

Bighorn sheep are widespread in the North American deserts though not truly abundant anywhere. In the United States, Arizona and Nevada have the largest populations (about 6,000 desert bighorn live in Arizona, and 5,000 in Nevada), followed by California (about 3,000) and Utah (2,500). Colorado, New Mexico, and Texas have less than 500 each (Toweill and Geist, 1999). Baja California has an estimated 2,500 desert bighorns, and Sonora has about 2,000. Reintroductions of deseert bighorn sheep to historic ranges in Mexico s Chihuahuan Desert have been made only recently.

Wherever bighorn sheep exist, certain habitat elements are present. *Escape terrain*, an area of steep and rocky slopes or cliffs where bighorn sheep can escape from potential predators, is essential and located near feeding areas. More specifically, escape terrain usually consists of an area of at least twelve acres consisting of rock outcroppings, cliffs, or terraces, where the slopes have grades of at least twenty-five percent. Escape terrain is usually within three hundred yards of feeding areas for ewes, and one thousand yards for rams. Desert bighorn depend on vision to detect predators, so sheep usually select habitat that is very open with few shrubs or trees over thirty inches in height. A perennial source of water within two miles of large expanses of escape terrain is also preferred. It has been asserted by some wildlife managers that a minimum of 6.5 square miles of suitable habitat is the minimum habitat size for an individual bighorn (Singer and Gudorf, 1999).

Scientists and government agency personnel, when protecting bighorn and their habitat, have identified the need to establish a buffer zone at least ten miles wide to separate bighorn from areas where livestock is grazed (Singer and Gudorf, 1999). This buffer zone reduces the potential for transfer of diseases from domestic livestock (particularly domestic sheep) to wild bighorn. Domestic sheep have been selectively bred for centuries to increase their resistance to disease. As a result, even healthy domestic sheep can transfer bacteria to desert bighorns--bacteria that, in bighorns, cause pneumonia or even death. The buffer is also required to reduce the potential competition between desert bighorns and livestock for food, water, and space.

Desert bighorn sheep usually flee from human disturbance-- especially if that disturbance is not predictable. Although desert bighorns quickly become habituated to predictable events, like traffic on a highway, they do not become street smart. As a result, bighorns are often struck by automobiles where highways divide bighorn sheep habitat or travel routes.

The areas occupied by desert bighorn sheep are vast, and most include one or more semi-isolated mountains or mountain ranges (Toweill and Geist, 1999; U.S. Department of the Interior, 1988). Undisturbed desert bighorn sheep travel widely over the course of a

Bighorn Ewe

year, occasionally crossing even wide valleys into nearby mountain ranges to take advantage of the seasonal abundance of forage plants. Usually this involves moving from summer to winter ranges and back again. Over long periods of time these kinds of movements are thought to be essential for genetic interchange, through breeding, between the various herds that comprise what biologists refer to as a metapopulation.

Desert lands rarely support high numbers of bighorn sheep, and human development in valleys separating individual herds can isolate them, preventing the movement, interbreeding, and subsequent genetic exchange between animals of one range and another. This is thought to result in the loss of a bighorn population s vitality. So serious is this problem that wildlife biologists believe that an individual herd that numbers less than one hundred animals is at risk of extinction. As a consequence, the Bureau of Land Management (U.S. Department of the Interior, 1988), the National Park Service (Singer and Gudorf, 1999), and state wildlife agencies are developing plans to artificially move bighorn between mountain ranges and reintroduce bighorn into ranges where they have been extirpated.

Bighorn sheep habitat,
Ajo Mountains,
Organ Pipe Cactus National Monument,
Arizona.

Bighorn Food Plants

Mojave Yucca, *Yucca schidigera*

Desert Dandelion, *Maacothrix glabrata*

Mormon Tea, *Ephedra nevadensis*

Barrel Cactus, *Ferocactus cylindraceus*

Food

Desert vegetation is often scarce, and many plants secrete salts or toxins during portions of the year as a defense against grazing animals. Always adaptable, desert bighorn sheep have responded by becoming very selective feeders, choosing a wide range of grasses, shrubs and forbs but only during certain seasons (Monson and Sumner, 1980).

Grasses such as galleta, needlegrass, grama grasses, and bluegrasses are especially important. However, though grasses are nutritious and generally digestible, the breakdown of grasses during digestion produces less metabolic water than found in other species of plants. Therefore desert bighorns must contend with a nearly constant need for obtaining water from their environment.

Shrubs are also very important in the diet of desert bighorn sheep. Some of these may be eaten only at certain times of the year, or during particular stages of plant growth. Among the plants important in the diet of bighorn sheep at higher elevations in the Mojave Desert are sagebrush, Mormon tea, mountain mahogany, scrub oak, blackbrush and winterfat. At lower elevations yuccas are included in the diet. In the Sonoran Desert jojoba and mesquite are important wherever they occur, with catclaw, whitethorn, ironwood, and palo verde somewhat less important. Mormon tea, brittlebush, and silverbush are seasonally utilized. In addition to these plants, silktassel, sotol, agave, sacahuista, and soapbush are important in Chihuahuan Desert habitats. Cacti, particularly prickly pear and barrel cactus, are also important foods in some areas, with several reports that desert bighorn sheep select these plants for their water content. Recent studies, however, have shown that the pulp of these cacti may contain such a high content of mineral salts that little free water can be gained by consuming these species.

Desert bighorn sheep also consume many species of small forbs that are available only during short periods of the year. These annual species include Indian wheat, filaree, globe mallow, euphorbia, spineflower, and peppergrass.

Perennial bunch grass - bighorn food

Behavior

Perhaps the best-known behavior associated with desert bighorn sheep is the clash of horns as rams of equal horn size batter each other, head to head. The resultant "crack" can often be heard for miles. This behavior is most commonly associated with the rut (the breeding period for desert bighorn sheep) which begins in late June and typically reaches its peak in July or August. Rams with the largest horns are dominant and do most of the breeding. As a consequence, two rams of nearly equal horn size may clash for hours until a victor emerges. By the same token, fights don't often occur between rams of unequal horn size, since rams literally size each other up before doing battle (Geist, 1971).

Breeding activity is associated with traditional rainy seasons. The resultant increase in forage may improve the physical condition of ewes, increasing the likelihood of successful breeding. Because climate seems to play a major role in the timing of the rut, rutting activity occurs at different times in different places. In the relatively cold northern ranges it occurs in July but may continue into December in the more southerly ranges.

Rams and ewes live apart most of the year. Among rams, the largest-horn animals are nearly always dominant. Rams tend to

An old and a young ram meet. Dominance is decided by horn size.

travel the greatest distances to seek out the best feeding areas. Rams that are most successful in locating high-quality food grow the largest horns. As a result, these large rams displace smaller rams for favored feeding or resting sites. They are also successful in discouraging competitors from challenging them for the favors of receptive ewes during the breeding season (Geist, 1971).

Unlike rams, ewes spend most of their lives in close proximity to rugged cliffs–places of security for their lambs. When the horns of young rams begin to develop the massiveness typical of males (at two years of age), they are expelled from the ewe groups. These young rams search for larger-horned males, and when they find such a ram (or band of rams), they join them in their wanderings.

Reproduction and Growth

Lambs are born following a gestation period of six months.
Although they can be born at any time of year, in those areas where
the rut peaks in July or August the lambing peak typically occurs in
January or February--the time when forage for lactating ewes is
most abundant. There is also a tendency for lambs to be born later,
through June, in the southern portion of the range. This reflects the
likelihood of summer rain and the growth and blossoming of plants
during the Sonoran Desert summer.

Ten to fourteen days prior to birth, a maternal ewe leaves the band
to locate an isolated rocky hideaway. This is where the lamb is born
and where it spends the first few days of life. (Twin lambs are
extremely rare among desert bighorn sheep.) A young lamb is
precocious and usually stands within minutes after birth. Within a
few days it is scrambling among the cliffs, following its mother
everywhere.

Ewes and their lambs typically rejoin the maternal herd within a
week (two at most) following birth. As more and more ewes bring
their new lambs into the herd a *nursery group* forms. This group
often spends the night high up on rocky ridges, away from potential
predators. During the daylight hours the ewes cautiously descend to

lower elevations as they seek the most succulent forage. Near the bottom, the lambs are often left to gambol about a rocky outcrop in the care of a few older ewes. The majority of ewes continue to the less secure canyon floors or alluvial fans where they feed most of the day. In the late afternoon the ewes return to their lambs, again leading them to high ridges to spend the night.

Mother s milk is the only food consumed by a lamb in its first two or three weeks of life. After that it eats ever-increasing amounts of vegetation--usually plant species observed to be eaten by its mother. Weaning occurs at around six months and can be very stressful. Many lambs do not survive the loss of milk in their diet if forage conditions are unfavorable.

A ewe and her newborn lamb.

A ewe and her ten-month-old lamb.

The age of a lamb can be estimated by the growth of its horns. No horns are present until about two months of age. By four months horns appear as small hard bumps. At six months horns are roughly triangular in side view.

Although desert bighorn sheep may be sexually mature at six months of age, physical maturity is not normally reached until two and half years for ewes, and three and a half years for rams.

Competition

Deer are the only other large native grazing animal in desert mountains but they generally do not occupy the steep terrain favored by bighorn. Deer are more often found in the flatlands between ranges. Only the diminutive white-tailed deer in the eastern Sonoran and Chihuahuan deserts typically shares habitat with desert bighorn.

The scarcity of vegetation and water in desert habitats means that competition for resources can be intense. Deer are typically browsers, selecting shrubs over grasses. Bighorn sheep, however, also rely heavily on shrubs including legumes such as catclaw, white-thorn, ironwood, palo verde, mesquite and fairyduster. Thus there is a potential for food competition, particularly when mule deer and bighorn sheep are forced to winter together. Mule deer, because of their greater size and reach, are likely to out-compete desert bighorn sheep for food in such situations.

There is also the potential for deer to compete with bighorn for water. Bighorn, however, are capable of living for long periods without drinking water. They are thus able to survive in many regions where water resources are limited. Deer cannot live in desert areas where reliable drinking water is not present.

Much more serious is competition with feral burros. (Domestic animals living wild are said to be feral.) While burros favor rolling

Mule deer, Odocoileus hemionus,
Joshua Tree National Park, California.

hills and rarely use the steep terrain favored by bighorn, the two animals eat many of the same plant species. In addition, burros eat many kinds of plants that bighorns cannot effectively digest. Burros are also larger and so require more food. Whereas bighorn usually nibble and move on, burros often devour entire plants, roots and all. As a result of the burros eating habits, they can reduce the amount of food available to bighorn sheep. Burros also drink much larger amounts of water than do bighorn and tend to concentrate around waterholes. This discourages bighorn from using waterholes used by burros. Finally, burros have the potential to increase their numbers in a given area very rapidly. They lack predators and do not succumb to disease as readily as do bighorn. When all three of these factors are combined, it is evident that burros have the potential to sharply reduce or even eliminate desert bighorn sheep in a given area (Seegmiller and Ohmart, 1981).

In addition to burros, domestic livestock may also compete for the food and water required by desert bighorn. Much larger than bighorn, cattle and horses require far more food each day, and even seasonal grazing by such animals in desert environments can reduce the amount of food available to bighorns. Domestic sheep pose the most serious problem on bighorn sheep ranges. Not only do domestic sheep compete directly for food and water, but due to their close evolutionary relationship with bighorn, domestic sheep carry diseases and parasites that can decimate bighorn sheep populations. Most biologists have concluded that it was the introduction of domestic sheep into desert bighorn ranges (along with the resultant competition for food and water, and the transmission of domestic sheep diseases to wild bighorns) that resulted in the widespread loss of wild sheep populations between 1870 and 1945 (Singer and Gudof,1999; Toweill and Geist, 1999).

Wild burro, Equus asinus,
a competitor of bighorn sheep.

Mortality

Most people immediately think of predators when they consider causes of mortality among desert bighorn sheep. In fact, bighorn are subject to many different kinds of mortality, particularly during the first year of life. Typically, not even half of the lambs born each year survive to their first birthday—a number that may be reduced further in unusually harsh years.

New-born lambs, though precocious, are naive about their environment and some portion of each year's lamb crop is lost due to accidents. Some fall from cliffs, others twist a leg, still others may drown at steep-sided waterholes. Accidents also affect adults, who may fall while attempting to escape predators or be struck by vehicles when crossing highways.

Diseases and parasites also take an annual toll on bighorn sheep numbers, particularly when the sheep are stressed. Desert bighorn appear to be especially subject to bacterial pneumonia, and many herds have experienced a dramatic die-off following exposure to bacterial agents carried by apparently healthy domestic sheep. Bluetongue, a viral disease that can be transmitted between bighorn sheep and livestock by insects, is nearly always fatal. Other diseases and parasites debilitate and stress bighorn, contributing to their death. Such problems include infestations by ticks (that can cause anemia), mites (that can produce scabies or mange), and the nose bot fly (whose larvae can cause chronic sinusitis).

Desert bighorn sheep are preyed on by many species. Golden eagles can be effective predators of lambs which they snatch from rocky cliffs or harry until the young animals fall to their death. Wild cats (bobcats, mountain lions, and even the rare jaguar) are at home in the rocky habitats selected by desert bighorn sheep, and may kill both lambs and adults. Mountain lions, in particular, are believed to select bighorn sheep as prey items in some desert mountain ranges. Coyotes and wolves are less at home in steep and rocky terrain, but will kill bighorns when they can catch them away from secure habitat.

Despite all of these dangers, perhaps the greatest risk affecting desert bighorn sheep survival is climate. Desert habitats are harsh, and extended drought can deny herds the food and water necessary for survival. Winter storms can rob their bodies of heat. Desert bighorns have adapted specialized mechanisms for dealing with these problems, but the survival of individuals can still be overwhelmed by unusual events. The best insurance humans can provide for desert bighorn sheep is not the elimination of predators, or even diseases, but the protection of large blocks of suitable habitat, free from competition with feral animals. Also important are travel corridors between mountain ranges, allowing meta-populations to exist.

Bighorn Predators

Coyotes have been known to attack and kill bighorn lambs. There are also records of two or more coyotes attacking adult bighorn.

Golden eagles can be effective predators of lambs which they may snatch from rocky cliffs or harry until young animals fall to their death.

Impact of Humans

Desert bighorn sheep were very important to Indians, probably since Indians first arrived in the American southwest approximately 12,500 years ago (Valdez and Krausman, 1999). Indians hunted desert bighorns for their meat as well as for their hides, horns and bones. Hides were used for clothing and bags, and horns were used to make a wide variety of knives, spoons, digging sticks, bows, and ornaments. Bones were used for scrapers, awls and other implements (Cornett, 2000).

The significance of desert bighorn sheep to Southwest Indians is indicated by a tremendous volume of rock art. Bighorn are featured in petroglyphs and pictographs throughout the entire southwest desert region. In California s Coso Mountains, more than half of the ten thousand documented petroglyphs depict bighorn sheep (Grant in Monson and Sumner, 1980). While the intent behind such images is unknown, archaeologists have speculated that images were designed (perhaps by medicine men called shamans) to bring about hunting success. Another theory asserts that the Shoshone peoples believed bighorn sheep were keepers of the rain, able to control the release of moisture from the underworld. By this theory, depictions of desert bighorn sheep might be viewed as pleas for rain (Toweill and Geist, 1999).

Bighorn petroglyph
Coso Ranges, California

Bighorn sheep were also venerated as deities by many Southwest tribes. The Sand Papago believed that bighorn sheep controlled the wind, and early accounts tell of great piles of bighorn sheep horns near waterholes to ensure that the wind did not leave. Bones were burned to quiet the spirits of the animals killed, so that the remaining bighorns would not leave the area (Grant in Monson and Sumner 1980). The important Humpbacked god of the Navajo, *Ganaskidi*, is always portrayed as having the horns of a bighorn sheep, and may have been 'borrowed' by the Navajo from the Hopi bighorn sheep kachina, *Panwu*. Hopi fetishes carved of stone or bone were believed to provide the owner good luck.

Desert bighorn were first brought to the attention of Europeans in the 16th century. Spaniards intent on plundering the riches of the Aztec Empire no doubt encountered desert bighorn sheep during their explorations. Desert bighorn sheep were mentioned in journals kept by Francisco Vasquez de Coronado during his search, in 1540, for the Seven Cities of Cibola. A note on the early abundance of desert bighorn sheep in what is presently New Mexico was provided by Don Juan de Onate about 1600, who wrote that the area was " plentiful in meat of buffalo, sheep with huge antlers, and native turkey" (Graham in Monson and Sumner, 1980).

The Spanish explorers and colonizers frequently hunted desert bighorns (particularly near waterholes) as did the Indians before them. Populations of desert bighorn, however, were probably not significantly affected by hunting (if at all) until after the Civil War, when huge numbers of U.S. citizens sought wealth and opportunity out West.

*Bighorn ram and
ewe (upper left*

The invasion of desert habitats by large numbers of people searching for mineral wealth and establishing homesteads after the Civil War brought about the near-complete demise of desert bighorn sheep populations between 1870 and 1945. Market hunting was one factor that reduced populations of bighorn sheep, but even more serious was the introduction of domestic livestock on critical bighorn sheep ranges. Unregulated grazing by cattle, domestic sheep, and burros removed forage from lands that had provided habitat for bighorn sheep populations, and domestic livestock diseases ravaged the surviving bighorn herds. By the beginning of the twentieth century, even ardent conservationists were nearly certain that desert bighorn sheep, as well as many other species of native wildlife, were doomed to extinction. That this prediction did not come to pass was due in large part to President Theodore Roosevelt and his bold new concept of setting aside large blocks of federal land in parks, reserves, and national forests for wildlife.

The past century has been witness to the restoration of desert bighorn sheep in many areas from which they had entirely disappeared. Efforts of conservationists and sportsmen's groups, working in cooperation with state wildlife management agencies and federal land management agencies have doubled the number of desert bighorn sheep in the United States since 1950 (Toweill and Geist, 1999). Although many populations are still at dangerously low levels, an increasing understanding of population requirements and habitat management practices is helping secure the future of this magnificent species.

Herd of young Peninsular rams and ewes,
San Jacinto and Santa Rosa Mountains
National Monument, California.

Where to View Desert Bighorn

Desert bighorn sheep are very sensitive to human intrusion and viewing them can often be difficult. In some areas, however, bighorn are habituated to the routine activities of humans and do not perceive human presence as a threat. In such places bighorn can be approached quite closely. In any situation, however, it is best to not approach bighorn on foot. They are likely to flee, expending energy needed for their survival in harsh desert environments.

Many state and national parks in the Southwest have thriving herds of desert bighorn, and most have identified vantage points from which they may commonly be seen. Some of the best sites are the interface of desert environments and reservoirs or lakes–attractive to desert bighorns because of the availability of water. Desert bighorns have become very acclimated to humans in boats and rafts at many of these areas, affording excellent viewing opportunities. A few of the better-known sites are listed below.

Arizona
Glen Canyon National Recreation Area
Over eight hundred animals roam the shorelines of Lake Powell. The lake is at the center of the recreation area and bighorn sheep are regularly seen from boats on the reservoir.

The Grand Canyon - one of the best places to see bighorn.

Grand Canyon National Park - This national park is the best place in the nation to observe desert bighorn sheep. In particular, bighorns have become habituated to rafts on the Colorado River, allowing visitors to pass by and view them at close range.

California
Anza-Borrego Desert State Park
Located south of Palm Springs and southwest of California's Salton Sea, Anza-Borrego Desert State Park is home to the endangered Peninsular desert bighorn sheep. Bighorn are often observed in Borrego Palm Canyon just west of the park visitor center.

Death Valley National Park
Desert bighorn sheep are found throughout most of the mountain ranges and rocky outcrops surrounding Death Valley. Populations are small, however, and animals are often difficult to locate.

Santa Rosa-San Jacinto Mountains National Monument
Peninsular bighorn are doing poorly in this monument that lies on the southern edge of Palms Springs and the Coachella Valley. Nevertheless, they can still be observed in the mountains above the cities of Rancho Mirage and Palm Desert and occasionally crossing Highway 74.

Nevada
Desert National Wildlife Range
Easily accessible from Las Vegas, the Desert National Wildlife Range provides good habitat for desert bighorn sheep.

Bighorn often come to drink at the bottom of Borrego Palm Canyon in Anza-Borrego Desert State Park, California

Lake Mead National Recreation Area - Adjoining Arizona's Grand Canyon National Park, this area is heavily used by boaters. Visitors often see some of the estimated one thousand desert bighorn sheep on rocky ridges near the lakeshore.

Utah

Arches and Canyonlands National Parks - These two parks provide habitat for over six hundred desert bighorns sheep. Desert bighorns have become habituated to vehicle traffic along the heavily traveled road corridor. Bighorns may also be seen from major hiking trails, and major concentrations are found along the Colorado River.

Capitol Reef National Park - This national park contains a growing herd of about 150 desert bighorns, located primarily in the central and southern portions of the park.

Zion National Park - Desert bighorn sheep are found in the southern portions of the park and southward to Canaan Mountain.

Face of a ram

BIBLIOGRAPHY

Cornett, J.W. 2000. *Indians and desert animals.* Nature Trails Press, Palm Springs, California.

Geist, V. 1971. *Mountain sheep: a study in behavior and evolution.* The University of Chicago Press, Chicago, Illinois.

Geist, V. 2000. *Antelope country.* Krause Publications, Iola, Wisconsin.

Krausman, P.R., J.R. Morgart, and M. Chilelli. 1984. *Annotated bibliography of desert bighorn sheep literature, 1897-1983.* The Southwest Natural History Association, Phoenix, Arizona.

Monson, G., and L. Sumner. 1980. *The desert bighorn: its life history, ecology and management.* University of Arizona Press, Tucson, Arizona.

Nabhan, G.P. 1993. *Counting sheep: twenty ways of seeing desert bighorns.* The University of Arizona Press, Tucson, Arizona.

Seegmiller, R.F., and R.D. Ohmart. 1981. Ecological relationships of feral burros and desert bighorn sheep. Wildlife Monographs 78, The Wildlife Society, Washington, D.C.

Singer, F.J., and M.A. Gudorf. 1999. Restoration of bighorn sheep populations in and near fifteen national parks: conservation of a severely fragmented species. U.S. Geological Survey open file report 99-102, Fort Collins, Colorado.

Toweill, D.E., and V. Geist. 1999. *Return of royalty: wild sheep of North America.* Boone & Crockett Club, Missoula, Montana.

U.S. Department of the Interior. 1988. Rangewide plan for managing habitat of desert bighorn sheep on public lands. Washington, D.C.

U.S. Fish and Wildlife Service. 2000. Recovery plan for bighorn sheep in the peninsular ranges, California. Ecological Services, Region 1, Portland, Oregon.

Valdez, R., and P.R. Krausman. 1999. *Mountain sheep of North America.* University of Arizona Press, Tucson, Arizona.

About the author . . .

Dale Toweill received his B.S., M.S., and Ph.D. degrees in wildlife science and ecology. He has conducted research on many species of wildlife, and has written extensively. Some of his books include *Return of Royalty: Wild Sheep in North America* (Boone & Crockett Club), *Elk of North America* (Stackpole), *North American Elk Ecology and Management* (Smithsonian University Press), and *Perspectives on Biodiversity* (National Academy of Sciences).